Don't C
Make the Days Count

MW00412216

Ed Agresta

About the Author

Ed Agresta is an award-winning educator, lecturer, and coach. For over 30 years, he has been presenting his special insights into the most powerful techniques available for developing peak performance. He is a fascinating, humorous speaker and a gifted communicator, who has given more than 500 presentations to corporations, schools, and athletic teams.

Acknowledgments

All of the stories in this book are the result of my attending scores of seminars and sports clinics, listening to thousands of inspirational audiotapes, and reading hundreds of business and motivational books. I make no claim to being the original author of these stories.

So, to all the speakers and authors made an impact on my life, I say thank you. I hope I can pay homage by passing your stories and messages onto the next generation of speakers and doers.

I would like to acknowledge some very special people who have played a very important part contributing to my life and experiences:

My family – my wife, Kathy, my daughter, Jill, and my son, Todd. The success I've acknowledged as a teacher coach, speaker and now author would not have been possible without their support and loving concern. I thank you and love you more than you will ever know.

My dad, who had the ability to fix any car and who many times in the middle of the night, saved me when I was stuck. He taught me to give help when it was needed to treat all people with respect. I thank you and love you.

My mom, the loving disciplinarian of our household. The big wooden macaroni stick taught me that all situations have rules and regulations that must be followed. Lessons will always be remembered. I thank you and love you.

Acknowledgments

To my brother Ronald, how tough it must have been to be a younger brother to someone who was a real pain in the neck. I thank you for your patience and understanding. I love you.

My very special uncrowned champions: Dr. Robert Gilbert, the best of the best speakers and mentors, and Tony Dragona, someone who is always flexible and lives the "we can do that" life. I thank you and love you.

My quiet heroes who always say yes to life: Jerry Caputo, with his "you never give up" attitude; Celeste Barth, a true friend who has the ability to confront and defeat the F.F.U.D. Disease; and Marilyn Tiffany, someone who keeps her cool and stays classy when all craziness is going on around her. The examples they set for me and their other students cannot be expressed with mere words. I thank you and I love you.

I want to thank Irene Frankel and David Martin for their editorial and desktop publishing skills.

To LeeAnn Soriano (lasdesigns@live.com) part of my publishing "dream team" who took the vision of the book cover and wonderfully brought it to life.

And, last, but not least, I would like to thank the many coaches, players, parents, and students I've had the wonderful privilege of working with and learning from.

Contents

Contents

Introduction

We are the only creatures on this earth who know that our time here is limited. This life is our Super Bowl, NCAA National Championship, and Academy Awards Ceremony. Unless you know something I don't know, we're not coming back this way again. Our life is not a dress rehearsal (wouldn't it be nice if it were?). I guarantee that nobody reading (or not reading) this book will get out of this earth alive. A depressing thought if you're filling your life with time. An exciting thought if you're filling your time with life.

How many days do you think you live if you live to be 74 years old? (I hope we live to be 104 years old in good health.) Before you figure this out, take a guess between 100,000 and 200,000 days, Wrong! It's 27,010 days. Now I want you to multiply your age by 356 days and subtract this number from 27,010. Go ahead—do the math. Are you doing the most with your time?

Don't Count the Days...Make the Days Count, is about taking action and getting positive results. It's about helping you develop G.O.Y.A.—not Goya-brand products or the Spanish painter, but Get Off Your A--. There are 52 stories in this book. Read one story every week. Make a commitment to the commitment that you'll G.O.Y.A. one week at a time. This is the only way to achieve positive results.

How to Get the Most out of This Book

Using this book is a simple as 1-2-3.

1. Read one story every week. Then read what I say after each story. It's not right or wrong, but it is my power thought about the story.

2. Share the story with others and discuss it with them. This will bring up other points of view, which in turn, will help you create your own power thoughts—your ideas about the stories will motivate you or inspire you to take action. Write your power thoughts about the stories in the book.

3. Read over your power thoughts and write your action steps for the week. This is the step where people get lazy. Use the Triple A method: Become Aware of new information, pay Attention to the details, and then Attack the week with gusto.

Good luck!

Keep An Empty Head

Someone asked Albert Einstein, how many feet there were in a mile. "I don't know," Einstein replied. "Why should I fill my head with things like that, when I could look them up in a reference book in two minutes?"

Information is knowledge. Knowledge is potential power. Action is personal power.

Your Power Thoughts

_____

_____

_____

_____

_____

Your Action Steps

_____

_____

_____

_____

_____

You Know It's Going To Be A Bad Day When:

- You wake up face down on the pavement

- You call Suicide Prevention and they put you on hold.

- You see a 60 Minutes news team waiting in your office.

- Your birthday cake collapses from the weight of the candles.

- You want to put on the clothes you wore home from last night's party—and there aren't any.

- You turn on the news and they're showing emergency routes out of the city.

- Your twin forgets your birthday.

- You wake up to discover that your waterbed broke and then realize you don't have a water-bed.

- Your horn goes off accidentally and remains stuck as you follow a group of Hell's Angels on the freeway

The messenger of misery knocks on every door. Be aware, so you can prepare.

Your Power Thoughts

_____

_____

_____

_____

_____

Your Action Steps

_____

_____

_____

_____

_____

Pick-Up Sticks

A father called in his seven sons to instruct them in wisdom. He asked each son to go out and bring back two sticks. When they returned, the father took one stick at a time from each of the seven sons. He easily broke each single stick across his knee and tossed the parts away. He took the remaining seven sticks, bound them together as asked each son to try to break the bundle. No one could do it. "The lesson, my sons," the father related, "is this: Alone each of you is easily broken and defeated; together you are strong. Defeat is difficult when you are united as one body."

None of us is as strong as all of us.

Your Power Thoughts

Your Action Steps

The Oyster and the Eagle

When God made the oyster, He guaranteed him absolute social and economic security. The oyster's shell protects him from his enemies. When hungry, the oyster simply opens his shell and the food rushed in. He has no worries. He does not fight anyone. He doesn't go anywhere. He simply sits in his shell at the bottom of the water, pushed by the currents.

When God made the eagle, He gave him the sky as his domain. The eagle nests on the highest crag of the highest mountain, where storms threaten everyday. For food, he flies through miles of snow, rain, sleet, and wind. He screams out in defiance against the elements, but goes his way, building his own life. When attacked by an enemy, he is a vicious foe.

Accept the challenges so you may feel the exhilaration of victory.

Your Power Thoughts

_____

_____

_____

_____

_____

Your Action Steps

_____

_____

_____

_____

_____

The Eagle and the Rabbit

An eagle and a rabbit were standing at the edge of a deep gorge. The eagle flew to the other side, then turned and called to the rabbit, "Come on over! This view is better and there's plenty of food."

The rabbit thought to himself, "I have strong legs to help me leap and large ears to use as wings." So he took a running start and sprung into the air, only to fall to the bottom of the gorge.

The eagle looked down at the rabbit and called, "Perhaps you should have used the bridge!"

Your Power Thoughts

Your Action Steps

Look to Nature

A mother bird will know when it is time for her young to spread their wings and leave their nest for good. She knows when they are ready to fly. Some baby birds are timid and dare not leave the security of their nest. Others don't quite make up their minds. Soon the mother bird will stop coaxing them and actually push them out of the nest, for she knows they have the strength to fly if they want to. But look under the tree a day or two afterwards; sometimes you will find a dead bird or two – birds that just dropped to the ground without a struggle, birds that were too timid to struggle or even to try to fly. Their unwillingness to struggle was their mistake. Now they are dead. Those that struggled are alive.

Your Power Thoughts

Your Action Steps

Faith

A farmer heard reports that there was going to be terrible flood in his area. Police advised everyone to evacuate, but the farmer was determined to stay in his house.

As the water was rising, a police car came and offered to help him, but the farmer said, "No, I have faith."

As the water was getting higher, a man in a rowboat came by and offered to help, but the farmer said, "No, I have faith."

His house is now underwater, and the farmer was on top of his roof. A helicopter came and offered to save him, but the farmer said, "No, I have faith."

Just as he said that, a wave from a passing boat came. The farmer was knocked off the roof and drowned.

The next thing he knew he was up in heaven talking to God. He was very upset that God had saved him. He said how could you do this to me? I had complete faith in you,

"I don't understand why you're so upset," God answered, "I sent you a police car, a boat and a helicopter to save you."

Your Power Thoughts

_____

_____

_____

_____

_____

Your Action Steps

_____

_____

_____

_____

_____

Squares

How many squares do you see? Count them before you read on.

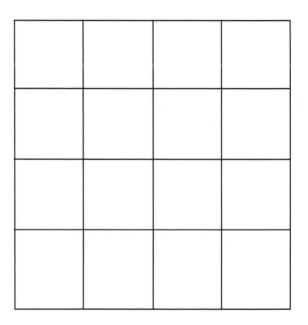

If you counted 16 or 17, you are in the majority of the people. If you counted 30, you are in the minority.

Your Power Thoughts

_____

_____

_____

_____

_____

Your Action Steps

_____

_____

_____

_____

_____

Push, Push, Push

A Texas billionaire made the following offer, to any young man with the courage and skills to swim across a swimming pool filled with alligators. He promised to give his daughter in marriage, a sports car, two oil wells, and a top position in his company.

On the big day, a large group of eligible young men gathered around the pool. Suddenly, one young man got into the water and swam like the blazes to the other side. The crowd went wild, clapping and cheering as the hero made his way across the pool. The rich father ran to his side, congratulated him, and then asked, "Which prize do you want first?"

First," the young man sputtered, "I want the name of the son-of-a-bitch who pushed me into the pool!"

Your Power Thoughts

_____

_____

_____

_____

_____

Your Action Steps

_____

_____

_____

_____

_____

Pulling Dust

In, 1901, H.C. Booth was sitting in a rocking chair on his front porch, watching the sunset. Living in the Midwest, he was also watching the dust blow. As he contemplated the scene, he wondered, "What if we could reverse the wind? Then, instead of blowing dust, we could pull dust."

Later that year, he went on to invent the vacuum cleaner.

The best question for creativity is, "What if?"

Your Power Thoughts

Your Action Steps

One Hop at a Time

Donald Bennett realized one of his lifelong dreams. He was the first amputee to climb Mount Rainier (14,410 Feet) on one leg. He had to make the climb twice, because the first year he attempted the climb he was stopped 410 feet from the summit by bad weather. Bennett never gave up, working out for one full year with only one thing on his mind: "I must get to the top." Then after five days of climbing, on July 15, 1988, Donald H. Bennett reached the top of Mount Rainier.

When asked how he did it, he explained, "One hop at a time. I imagined myself on the top of that mountain one thousand times a day in my mind. When I started to climb it, I just said to myself, 'anybody can hop from here to there. And I would. ' And when the going got toughest, and I was really exhausted, that's when I would look down at the path ahead and say to myself, 'You just have to take one more step and anybody can do this. And I would."

Focus X Belief + A Hop gets you to the top of your mountain.

Your Power Thoughts

_____

_____

_____

_____

_____

Your Action Steps

_____

_____

_____

_____

_____

Mosquitoes, Gnats, No See 'Ems, Elephants

Have you ever been bitten by a mosquito?

Have you ever been bitten by a gnat?

(Gnats are those little black things that get you.)

Have you ever been bitten by a "no see 'ems?
("No see 'ems" are things that bite you that you can't see, but you know they are there because you're scratching your arms.)

Have you ever been bitten by an elephant?

Take care of the little things, and the big things will take care of themselves.

Your Power Thoughts

Your Action Steps

Don't Forget to Take the Tie

Two men lost in the desert were about to die of thirst. As they crawled up and down the sand dunes, they saw a store. Not knowing if it was real or a mirage, they crawled up to the door and rang the bell. A man opened the door and asked what they wanted.

"Water, please," they replied.

The owner of the shop said, "We can give you ties. For water, you have to go to the restaurant three miles ahead."

"We don't need ties—we need water," said the two thirsty men. So off they crawled three more miles in the desert to the restaurant. When the got there, weak and about to die, the mustered enough strength and knocked on the door. "We need water. Please give us water," said the dying men.

The owner of the restaurant said, "I would gladly give you water, but I can't. You can't come in without a tie."

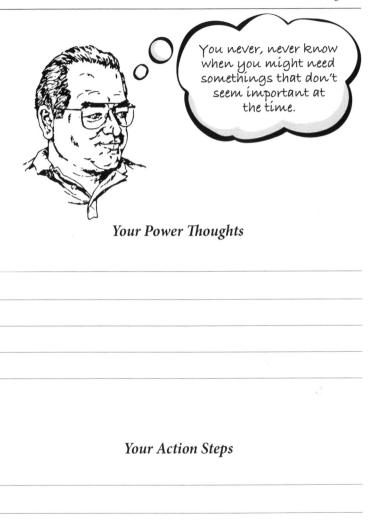

You never, never know when you might need somethings that don't seem important at the time.

Your Power Thoughts

Your Action Steps

Monks

Two monks had taken vows that they would never touch or even talk to women. On their way back to the monastery they came upon a stream. There they met a woman trying to get across. The older monk said. "May I help you?"

"Yes, thank you." said the woman. So the monk picked her up and carried her across.

The monks then continued on their way. Five hours later, they got to the monastery. The younger monk then said, "Do you know that you broke your vows? You spoke to and touched a woman."

"Yes, that's true," said the older monk, "but I carried her for 30 seconds, and you carried her five hours. Isn't it time to let go?"

Letting go will help you grow

Your Power Thoughts

_____

_____

_____

_____

_____

Your Action Steps

_____

_____

_____

_____

_____

Title

Monterey, California, used to be a paradise for pelicans. The local fishermen would clean their fish and throw the remains to the pelicans. The birds grew content, fat, and lazy. Eventually, however, the remains were put to commercial use, so the fishermen stopped feeding the pelicans.

The pelicans made no effort to fish for themselves. They wouldn't try to get food; they would just wait around. First, they became weak. Then they starved to death. They had forgotten how to fish for themselves.

Use it or lose it.

Your Power Thoughts

_____

_____

_____

_____

_____

Your Action Steps

_____

_____

_____

_____

_____

Last Could Be A Winner

More than 15,000 people compete in the New York City Marathon. It takes the winner a little over two hours to complete the race. The winner is met with the cheers of the crowd and the attention of the news reporters.

One particular year, the race started at 9:00 AM, and by 5:30 PM all 13,609 runners had completed the race except for one brave soul. At 9:30 PM, with no TV cameras, no one handing out water, and no one waving banners, the 13,610th person came across the finish line. Linden Dawn, her body bruised and cut, fell down across the finish line. She had completed the 26.2 miles on aluminum crutches. She had been born with cerebral palsy.

It's easy to finish anything. Just never, never quit.

Your Power Thoughts

_____

_____

_____

_____

_____

Your Action Steps

_____

_____

_____

_____

_____

Busting Loose

Elephants

The elephant in the circus is held by a weak little rope attached to its leg. Even though the adult elephant could snap the rope with one tug of his foot, he never tries. Why? Because when he was a little baby, his trainers wrapped a great big chain around his leg. After a few months of straining to get loose, the baby elephant finally gave up.

Fleas

Trained fleas can easily jump three to four feet off a table top, but they limit their jumps to only two or three feet in height. Why? Because the trainer kept them locked up in a box with a three-foot ceiling. Every time one of the fleas tried to jump out of the box, it would crash into the ceiling three feet above.

Barracuda

When a barracuda and a mackerel are in the same tank, the barracuda will eat the mackerel. As an experiment, some scientists put a clear plastic divider between the mackerel and the barracuda. Every time the barracuda tried to swim over to the mackerel, he would bump his nose against the invisible plastic shield. After a few days, the scientists removed the shield, leaving a clear path to the frightened mackerel. But the barracuda knew better. He knew from experience that it was "impossible" for him to swim to the other side.

Most invisible barriers are self imposed or imaginary

Your Power Thoughts

Your Action Steps

Hands, Hands, Hands

In the cartoon strip Peanuts, Linus is in the kitchen, eating a jelly sandwich. As he finishes the sandwich, it seems as if for the first time in his life he notices the hand that held the sandwich. He begins to admire first that hand, then the other hand, He tells himself that these great hands could be anything: a captain of industry, a great leader, a professional athlete, a skilled surgeon, a renowned novelist— even President of the United States!

Excited about his hands and the potential they hold, he runs into the next room where Lucy is watching TV and shouts, "Lucy! Lucy! Look at my hands!"

Lucy looks at his hands and then looks into his eyes an says, "They've got jelly on them."

If it is to be, it is up to me.

Your Power Thoughts

Your Action Steps

The Greatest Knowledge

A king asked his wife, Greta, to write down all the wisdom in the world. After five years she filled five books. The King was happy, but he asked her to make it simpler.

After five more years, Greta presented the king with just one book. The king, however, was still not satisfies. He asked her to come up with the one sentence that would give the people all the wisdom in the world.

Greta thought for a time and finally said, "There's no such thing as a free lunch."

Your Power Thoughts

_____

_____

_____

_____

_____

Your Action Steps

_____

_____

_____

_____

_____

Frogs

Two frogs accidentally fell into a bucket of cream. The first frog said, "We may as well give up. It's no use. There's no way out. We're goners."

"Keep on paddling," said the other frog. "We'll get out of this mess some how." The first frog began listing all the reasons they were doomed: "It's too thick to swim: it's to thin to jump out of; it's too slippery to crawl up. We're going to die." With that he gave up and drowned.

But the second frog kept on paddling. By morning, all the cream had turned into butter. He then hopped out and continues on his way.

Sink or swim. The decision is yours.

Your Power Thoughts

_____

_____

_____

_____

_____

Your Action Steps

_____

_____

_____

_____

_____

Go Fly a Kite

A young man flying a kite asked his father, "What holds the kite up?"

"The string," his dad replied.

"No, Dad, the string holds the kite down, not up."

The father replies, "If you think so, let go of the string."

The boy let go of the string and, sure enough, the kite began to fall. Isn't that strange? The very thing that happens to keep the kite down is actually what keeps it up.

Your Power Thoughts

Your Action Steps

"Failure" Sometimes Leads to Greatness

- Difficult child
- Less than one year of schooling
- Failed in business in '31
- Defeated for the legislature in '32
- Failed in business again in '33
- Elected to the legislature in '34
- Fiancée died in '35
- Defeated for Speaker in '38
- Defeated for Elector in '40
- Wife institutionalized in '42
- Only one of his sons lived past the age of 18
- Defeated for Congress in '43
- Elected to congress in '46
- Defeated for Congress in '48
- Defeated for Senate in '55
- Defeated for Vice President in '56
- Defeated for Senate in '58
- Elected President in 1860

This man was Abraham Lincoln.

When all else
fails,
try again.

Your Power Thoughts

_____

_____

_____

_____

_____

Your Action Steps

_____

_____

_____

_____

_____

E & E Factors

A man walked down the street was holding 100 one-dollar bills and two one-hundred-dollar bills. A strong wind came and blew all the money out of his hand. What should he pick up First? Pick up the one-dollar bills or look for and pick up the one-hundred-dollar bills?

If you pick up the one-dollar bills, you are efficient— you are doing the right thing. If you pick up the one-hundred-dollar bills, you are effective—you are doing things right.

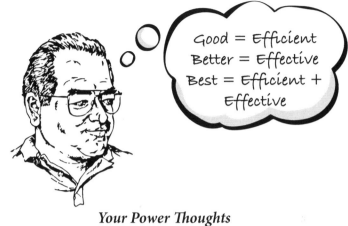

Good = Efficient
Better = Effective
Best = Efficient +
Effective

Your Power Thoughts

_____

_____

_____

_____

_____

Your Action Steps

_____

_____

_____

_____

_____

Dragons

All of us carry dragons on our backs. Dragons are big green ugly monsters that we can't see. We know they're there because the suck out our energy and make us negative. Some dragons that pull us down are "should," "ought to," bad habits, poor finances, routines, and some of our experiences.

To move forward, you must get the dragon off your back. Here's what to do: Pretend you're carrying a tray in front of you and make two fists. On the count of three, quickly snap your elbow back and knock these dragons off. (It's okay to smile and laugh. If you feel embarrassed, just close your eyes and no one will see you.)

Your Power Thoughts

_____

_____

_____

_____

_____

Your Action Steps

_____

_____

_____

_____

_____

Truth

One day, four high school students decided to cut their morning classes. After lunch, they reported to their teacher that their car had a flat tire. The teacher simply smiles and said' "Well you missed the test this morning, so take your seats and get out your notebooks."

Still smiling, she waited for them to settle down. Then she said, "First question. Which tire was flat?"

The truth is easier to remember than a lie.

Your Power Thoughts

Your Action Steps

Nothing Is As It Appears

Dear mom and Dad,

Since I left for college I've been remiss in writing to you. I'm really sorry for my thoughtlessness. I'll bring you up to date now, but before you read on, please sit down. You are not to read any further unless you're sitting down?

Well, then, I'm getting along pretty well now. The skull fracture I got when I jumped out of the window of my dormitory when it caught fire shortly after arrival here is pretty well healed. I spent only two weeks in the hospital, and now I can see almost normally and I get those sick headaches only once a day.

Fortunately, the fire in the dorm (and my jump) was witnessed by an attendant at the gas station near the dorm. He was the one who called the fire department and the ambulance. He also visited me in the hospital, and since I had nowhere to live because of the burnt-out dormitory, he was kind enough to invite me to share his apartment with him. It's really just a basement room, but it's kind of cute.

He's wonderful, and we've fallen deeply in love and are planning to get married. We haven't set the exact date yet, but it'll be before my pregnancy begins to show. Yes Mother and Dad, I am pregnant. I know how much you're looking forward to being grandparents, and I know you'll welcome the baby and give it the same love, devotion, and tender care you gave me when I was a child.

The reason for the delay in our marriage is that my boyfriend has a minor infection that's preventing us from passing our premarital blood tests, in which I carelessly caught from him. But I know you'll welcome him into our family with open arms. He's kind and although not well educated, he is ambitious. Although he's of a different race and religion from ours, I know you won't be bothered by that.

Now that I've brought you up to date, I want to tell you that there was no dormitory fire. I did not have a skull fracture. I was not in the hospital. I'm not pregnant. I'm not engaged. I'm not infected, and there's no boyfriend in my life. However, I am getting a D in history and as F in biology, and I wanted you to see these grades in their proper perspective.

Your loving daughter,
Nicole

Your Power Thoughts

Your Action Steps

The Swimmer

Mike loved to swim. Every day after school, he would go to the pool and swim lap after lap for pure enjoyment.

Mike became such a good swimmer that he decided to enter a ten-mile race across a lake. He practiced and practiced for the event.

Race day came and hundreds of contestants were there. Thousands of people came to cheer on their favorites.

Once the race started, Mike found himself in a commanding lead at the five-mile mark. At the eight-mile mark, however, Mike started to feel fatigued, and the second-place swimmer started to make his move.

At the nine-mile mark, the second swimmer was only thirty yards behind Mike. Mike knew it and pushed himself harder. With only five yards to go, the second-place swimmer passed Mike and won the race,

Even though Mike had lost the race, he was getting all the attention. He was confused. A lady who hadn't seen the race but was at the finish line was also confused. She couldn't see Mike but did know he had taken second place. She tapped a man on the shoulder and asked, "Why are the making such a big deal out of him" He didn't win!"

"No," replied the man, "but he would've easily won if he'd had two arms."

Your Power Thoughts

Your Action Steps

Puppies For Sale

A little boy walked past a pet store and read a sign that said, "Puppies for Sale." The boy walked into the store and asked, "How much are the puppies?" The store owner replied, "Fifty dollars." Putting his hand in his pocket, the boy pulled out some money. "I have five dollars," he said. "Can I look at them?"

The store owner smiled and whistled and from the back room came Lady, who ran down the store aisle followed by five teeny-tiny little balls of fur. One puppy could not keep up and was limping badly. The boy asked, "What's wrong with that little dog?"

The pet store owner explained that it had been born without a hip socket, so it would always be lame. The little boy became excited. "That's the puppy I want to buy!" he exclaimed. "That one?" asked the owner. "I'll give you that one for free." The little boy became angry and said, "That little dog is worth every bit as much as all the others, and I'll pay full price."

"You don't want to buy this little dog," said the owner. "He's never going to be able to run and jump and play with you like the rest of the puppies."

To this, the boy reached down and rolled up his pants leg to reveal a badly crippled left leg supported by a metal brace. He looked up at the store owner and softly replied, "Well, I don't run so well myself and this little puppy will need someone who understands."

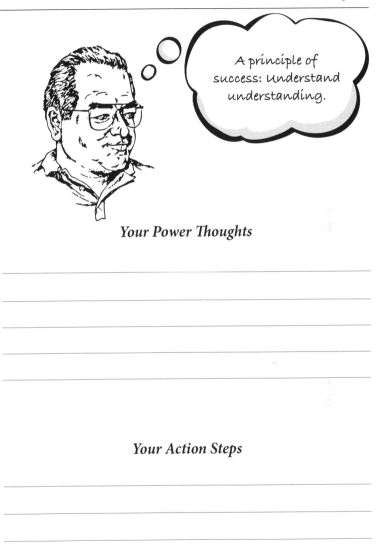

A principle of success: Understand understanding.

Your Power Thoughts

Your Action Steps

What Are You Looking At?

A college professor was giving a lecture about recession to a class. She placed a big sheet of white paper on the board. Then she made a black spot on the paper with her pencil and asked the student in the front row what he saw. The student replied quickly, "A black spot."

The professor asked every student the same question and each replied, "A black spot."

"Yes," the professor said, slowly. "Yes, there is a little black spot. But none of you saw the big sheet of white paper. And that's my lecture for today."

See the whole picture.

Your Power Thoughts

Your Action Steps

Watch Your Eyes

A little swallow was covering one eye with its wing, crying bitterly. An owl flew by and asked, "Little bird, what's wrong?"

The swallow pulled away its wing and showed a gash where once it had an eye.

"Now I understand," said the owl. "You're crying because the crow pecked out your eye!"

"No," replied the swallow, sadly. "I'm crying because I let him."

Your Power Thoughts

Your Action Steps

Wise Words

A king of long ago was searching for words of wisdom to help the people of his kingdom when they were plagued by worry and despair. He commanded his wise men to find the right words that would apply to every situation, every setback, and each despairing mood. After many years, they finally gave the king these four words: "This too shall pass."

Your Power Thoughts

_____

_____

_____

_____

_____

Your Action Steps

_____

_____

_____

_____

_____

Actions, Actions, Actions

Twelve members of a motorcycle gang went to a restaurant at a truck stop. There was only one customer, a truck driver who was finishing his meal. The gang members looked around, smiled at one another with cocky grins, then swaggered over to where the man sat. One bumped the truck driver's shoulder, another put out a cigarette on his plate, and several more joined in the taunting.

The truck driver just looked at them, stood up, went over to the cashier, paid for his meal, and then walked away.

The bikers really started laughing now, thoroughly enjoying themselves. The leader turned toward the cashier and said, "I thought truck drivers were supposed to be tough. That one sure isn't much of a man!"

"No," the cashier replied as he looked out the window. "And he's not much of a truck driver, either. He just backed over twelve motorcycles!"

Know when to speak up and when to shut up. Let your actions speak for you.

Your Power Thoughts

Your Action Steps

The Bear

Two men were walking together through a clearing in the woods when, suddenly, they spied a bear. Before the bear spotted them, one of the men ran as fast as he could and climbed a tree and hid. The other man wasn't as quick as his companion. He knew he couldn't escape, so he threw himself on the ground and pretended to be dead. The bear came up and sniffed all around him. The man held his breath. Finally, the bear went away.

After he was gone, the traveler in the tree came down and asked the other man what had happened. The second man told him the bear had walked all around him, and when he got close to his ear, the bear whispered to him. "He told me never to travel with a friend who'll leave you at the first sign of danger."

Surround yourself with others who believe in you and who are committed to your cause.

Your Power Thoughts

Your Action Steps

The Eagle and The Baby

Many years ago in Scotland, an eagle swooped down, picked up a baby, and carried it to the top of the mountain.

The greatest mountain climbers couldn't get up the side of the mountain.

Finally, to everyone's amazement, the mother of the child climbed the mountain, rescued the baby, and brought it back down the mountain.

Don't look for miracles. Make miracles.

Your Power Thoughts

Your Action Steps

Magnifying Glasses

Text A young child found a magnifying glass in his Cracker Jack box. His older friend told him he could do two things with this magnifying glass: he could burn ants, or he could direct the sun's rays onto a pile of dry leaves and start a fire.

The young boy decided to start a fire. Within a few minutes, he had burned down the whole house.

Focus is power.

Your Power Thoughts

_____

_____

_____

_____

_____

Your Action Steps

_____

_____

_____

_____

_____

Tennis Sneakers

Two men were hiking in the woods when they saw a bear in the distance coming toward them. One of the men stopped, took off his backpack, and began changing from his hiking boots into his tennis sneakers.

"What are you doing?" his friend asked in disbelief.

"You know you can't outrun that bear!"

"I know," the first man replied. "But I don't have to. I just have to outrun you."

Know who your competition is.

Your Power Thoughts

Your Action Steps

Spilled Milk

Many years ago, a science teacher used a simple, yet dramatic, demonstration to point out to his students how unproductive worry can be. He took a bottle of milk and smashed it into the sink, declaring, "Don't cry over split milk." He invited his students to gather around the sink to take a good look. "I want you to remember this lesson for the rest of your life," he said.

"That milk is gone. You can see it's down the drain, and all the fussing and hair pulling in the world won't bring back a single drop of it. All we can do is write it off, forget it, and go on to the next task."

The past doesn't equal the future.

Your Power Thoughts

Your Action Steps

Starfish

In Maine, they tell of an old man walking along the beach with his grandson.

The boy picked up each starfish they passed that was lying on the sand and threw it back in the ocean. "If I left them here," said the boy, "they would dry up and die. I'm saving their lives."

The old man said, "But the beach goes on for miles, and there are millions of starfish. What you're doing won't make any difference."

The boy looked at the starfish in his hand, threw it in the water, and answered, "It makes a difference to this one."

Your Power Thoughts

_____

_____

_____

_____

_____

Your Action Steps

_____

_____

_____

_____

_____

Give Up The Ropes

A farmer asked his neighbor if he might borrow a rope.

"Sorry," said the neighbor. "I'm using the rope to tie up my milk."

"You can't use rope to tie up milk," replied the bewildered farmer.

"I know," said the neighbor, "but when someone doesn't want to do something, one reason is as good as another."

Reason or results?

Your Power Thoughts

Your Action Steps

Three Riders

One night, three riders on horseback were out in the pitch black desert. As they rode, they heard a voice that said, "Get down off your horses and pick up what you feel. Put it in your saddle bags, and when daylight comes, you'll be both happy and sad.

The riders did what the voice commanded, and they patiently waited until sunrise. As the first rays of the sun came over the mountains, they jumped off their horses and emptied out their saddle bags. To their surprise, they saw emeralds, diamonds, rubies, and pearls.

They were happy because they had come that way and had heard the voice, but they were sad because they hadn't taken more.

You only come through this life once. Take all you can, while you can.

Your Power Thoughts

Your Action Steps

Excuses, Excuses

An elderly man in the hospital turned to his wife and said, "You know, Mary, I've been thinking ..."

"Yes?" she replied.

"You know, we've been married for 45 years now ..."

"Yes?" she replied.

"Remember the first year we were married? We had a bad crop and lost half the farm, and there you were, right by my side."

"Yes," she replied.

"That second year, we had another bad crop and lost the other half of the farm. And you were right by my side."

"Yes," she replied.

"Then we started five businesses and all five of them failed, and there you were right by my side."

"Yes," she replied.

"Now here I am in the hospital, terminally ill, and the doctors don't expect me to walk out of here alive. And here you are, right by my side."

"Yes," she replied.

"You know, Mary, I've been thinking ... You're bad luck!"

When you point your finger at someone else, your three other fingers point back at you.

Your Power Thoughts

_____

_____

_____

_____

_____

Your Action Steps

_____

_____

_____

_____

_____

Caterpillars To Butterflies

A metamorphosis is a total change in form.

In Stage 1, it is an egg on a leaf.

In Stage 2, it is an ugly caterpillar. It gives off an offensive odor, and has hairs that sting.

In Stage 3, it spins a cocoon about itself.

In Stage 4, it frees itself from the cocoon. It has become a butterfly, a beautiful creature of nature.

Your Power Thoughts

Your Action Steps

Let Me Have Air

One day a young man asked Socrates, "How can I obtain great success?"

Socrates casually led the young man into a river. Then he put his hand on the young man's head and plunged him into the water. Socrates held him down. The young man struggled, temporarily freed himself, and gasped for air, but Socrates quickly held him under again.

Finally, Socrates let the young man up. Amazed and bewildered, not to mention soaked and scared, the young man said, "What's the matter with you? I asked you how to acquire success and you tried to kill me!"

"When you need success as much as you want air," Socrates replied, "you will achieve it."

Do whatever it takes.

Your Power Thoughts

_____

_____

_____

_____

_____

Your Action Steps

_____

_____

_____

_____

_____

Plane Flight

Whenever you take a plane, the flight attendant will give you instructions about what to do in an emergency. She will tell you, "If there is a loss of cabin pressure, the oxygen mask will come down from the compartment above your head." She then will tell you to place it over your nose and mouth, securing it tightly.

Next she will give you the most important instructions of all: "If you are traveling with a young child, put your mask on first so that you are strong enough to take care of your child."

Your Power Thoughts

Your Action Steps

Don't Be A Jerk

A man went to his friend's house. While there, he went into the yard next door where there was a dog. The dog ran up to him and bit him on the leg. Whose fault was it that the man was bitten? That's right, it was the dog's fault because the man didn't know that the dog would bite.

The next day the man went back to his friend's house. Again he went into the yard next door, and again the same dog bit him. Whose fault was it now?

That's right, it was the man's fault. When you get bitten by a dog the first time, it's not your fault because you don't know the dog would bite. If you go in the same backyard and get bitten by the same dog again, you're a jerk.

There are no mistakes...only feedback and adjustments.

Your Power Thoughts

Your Action Steps

One Bite At A Time

Person A: I'm so hungry, I could eat an elephant!
Person B: How do you eat an elephant?
Person A: One bite at a time.

Inch by inch, is a cinch. Yard by yard, it's hard.

Your Power Thoughts

_____

_____

_____

_____

_____

Your Action Steps

_____

_____

_____

_____

_____

After Playing Outside All Day

Young Todd asked his mother, "Mom, if I fell out of a tree, would you rather I break my leg or tear my pants?"

"What a silly question," his mother replied. "Tear your pants, of course."

"Well, I've got good news, Mom. I've torn my pants."

All results have consequences.

Your Power Thoughts

_____

_____

_____

_____

_____

Your Action Steps

_____

_____

_____

_____

_____

Processionary Caterpillars

Fabre, a French naturalist, conducted an unusual experiment with some processionary caterpillars. These caterpillars blindly follow the one in front of them, hence, the name.

Fabre carefully arranged them in a circle around the rim of a flowerpot so that the lead caterpillar actually touched the last one, making a complete circle. In the center of the flowerpot, he put pine needle, which is food for the processionary caterpillar. The caterpillars started around this circular pot. Around and around they went, hour after hour, day after day. For seven full days, they went around the flowerpot. Finally, they dropped dead of starvation and exhaustion with an abundance of food less than six inches away.

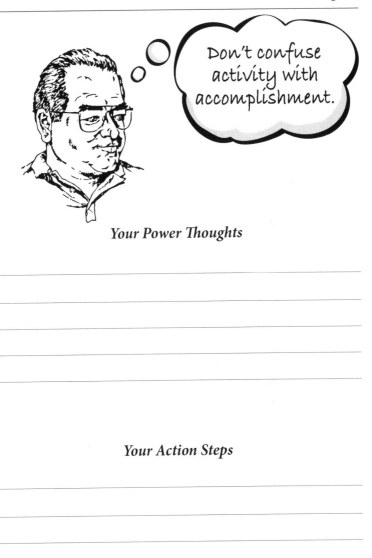

Don't confuse activity with accomplishment.

Your Power Thoughts

Your Action Steps

Legs

A man trained a flea to jump on command. Every day, the man pulled out one of the flea's six legs. Every day, with one more leg gone, the insect had more difficulty jumping. When the man removed the sixth leg, he said, "Jump!" but the flea, of course, couldn't move. "This simply shows that when you remove all the legs from a flea, the flea becomes deaf," the man observed.

Jumping to conclusions is the only exercise some people get.

Your Power Thoughts

Your Action Steps

Get in the Wheelbarrow

Phillipe, a world-famous aerialist from France, had just completed a tightrope walk across Niagara Falls in less than ideal conditions. It was a windy day, and instead of a balance pole, he used a wheelbarrow filled with rocks. When he got safely to the other side, he was met by cheering admirers. One of the spectators asked Phillipe if he thought he could go back across. Phillipe replied, "I feel very fortunate to have accomplished this feat."

But the man asked again, "Do you think you can go back across?"

Phillipe, annoyed at the repeated question, asked the inquiring man, "Do you believe I can go back across?" "Yes," the man replied. "I believe you can." After hearing the man's answer, Phillipe went over to the wheelbarrow, dumped out the rocks, and said, "If you truly believe that I can go back across, then get in this wheelbarrow."

Positive believing and positive thinking. There is a difference.

Your Power Thoughts

Your Action Steps

Mountain Top

In Japan, there is a place on a flat-topped mountain surrounded by a dense forest called, "The place you leave your parents." It's where children leave their parents when it's time for them to die.

One day, a man was carrying his mother up the mountain, for they both knew it was her time to leave this world. As they went, the old woman was breaking branches off the trees. The son asked, "Mother, what are you doing?" His mother replied, "I'm breaking these for you so that after you leave me, you'll know your way back."

True love is unconditional.

Your Power Thoughts

Your Action Steps

Just Look In Your Hands

Once, a long time ago, a wise man was coming to town to answer any questions the townspeople had. The whole town was looking forward to the day.

Two smart aleck boys were going to try to discredit the wise man by asking him a question he couldn't answer. Then all the townspeople would laugh at the wise man and run him out of town. This was their plan: They were going to put a little bird in their hands, and ask the wise man if the bird was alive or dead. If the wise man said it was dead, they would open up their hands and it would fly away. If he said it was alive, they would snap its neck and show everyone a dead bird. Either way, the wise man would be wrong.

The day finally came and the whole town gathered around the wise man. The two boys waited their turn and then asked, "Wise man, is this bird in our hands alive or dead?"

The wise man, being intelligent, waited for a moment. Then he looked the boys right in the eyes and said, "My children, whether the bird is alive or dead depends on you-the power is in your hands."

Your Power Thoughts

_____

_____

_____

_____

_____

Your Action Steps

_____

_____

_____

_____

_____

Other titles by Ed Agresta

Power Statements
Power Statements are statements which can be used for communicating, inspiring, motivating and teaching. Power Statements will lead, guide and direct you from where you are, to where you want to be.

I Dare You *A Guide to Successful Living*
Become successful and selfconfident with "DARES" that will transform your life. Your first dare— say "YES" out loud, I DARE YOU...

W.O.W. *Watch Out World*
WOW= **W**atch **O**ut **W**orld, here I come, is a book which will lead, guide, and direct you to success. Short, powerful strategies and techniques that will help you everyday to take another step toward your WOW life.

TO:
- Contact Ed Agresta
- Get information or order copies of this book or other titles by Ed Agresta
- Schedule Ed Agresta to give his talk to your group or organization

e-Mail:
DontCountTheDays@live.com

**POWER THOUGHTS
HOTLINE
24/7
609-660-8156**

2497308R00060

Made in the USA
San Bernardino, CA
29 April 2013